THE FOURPOSTER

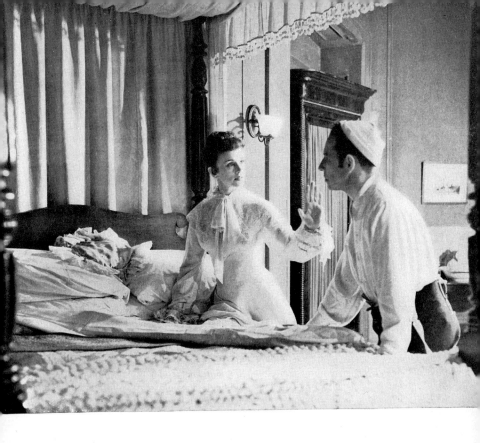

THE
FOURPOSTER

by

JAN DE HARTOG

RANDOM HOUSE, NEW YORK

THE FOURPOSTER *was first presented by The Playwrights' Company at the Ethel Barrymore Theatre, New York City, on Wednesday, October 24, 1951, with the following cast:*

AGNES   Jessica Tandy

MICHAEL   Hume Cronyn

Directed by José Ferrer

Setting by Syrjala

Costumes by Lucinda Ballard

SCENES

ACT ONE

SCENE I: 1890.
SCENE II: A year later.

ACT TWO

SCENE I: 1901.
SCENE II: Seven years later.

ACT THREE

SCENE I: 1913.
SCENE II: Twelve years later

ACT ONE

ACT ONE

Scene I

1890. Night.

Bedroom. Fourposter. Door in back wall, window to the right, washstand and low chair to the left. The room is dark. Low-burning gas lamps shimmer bluishly to the right of arch and at bed, left.

The door is opened clumsily, and HE *enters, carrying* HER *in his arms into the room out of the lighted passage.* HE *wears a top hat on the back of his head;* SHE *is in her bridal gown.* HE *stops in the moonlight, kisses her, whirls and carries her to bed.*

SHE

Oh, Micky, whoo! Hold me! Hold me tight! Whoo! Whoo! I'm falling. I can't . . . (HE *throws her onto the bed and tries to kiss her again*) Michael, the door! The door! (HE *runs to the door and closes it.* SHE *gets off the bed, straightens her hat and dress*) Oh, goodness, my hair . . . and look at my dress! (SHE *turns on the gas bracket on wall beside the bed.* HE *goes to her, takes off gloves, puts one in each pocket and kneels before her*) What are you doing?

HE

I'm worshipping you.

3

SHE

Get up immediately! (*Tries to lift him up*) Michael, get up, I say!

HE

Can't I worship you?

SHE

Are you out of your senses? If our Lord should see you . . .

HE

He could only rejoice in such happiness.

SHE

Michael, you mustn't blaspheme, you know you mustn't. Just because you've had a little too much to drink . . .

HE

I haven't drunk a thing. (*Teeters on his knees*) If I'm drunk, I'm drunk only with happiness . . .

SHE

You wouldn't be praying with everything on if you weren't. (*Turns*) Oh! Goodness! I think I am too.

HE

Happy?

SHE

Tipsy. Let me see if I can stand on one leg. (*Holding her hands out to him, tries and fails*) Whoo!

HE
(*Rises*)

Angel!
(*Tries to kiss her, but* SHE *dodges*)

SHE

Michael, that hat . . .

HE

What? Oh. (*Takes hat off*) What have you got in your hand?

SHE

A little rose . . . a little rose from our wedding cake.

HE

Let's eat it.

SHE

No—I want to keep it—always . . .
(SHE *puts it in her dress.* HE *puts hat on.*)

HE

Agnes . . . tell me that you are happy.

SHE

Please, Michael, do say something else for a change.

HE

I can't. I've only one word left to express what I feel: happy.
Happy, happy, happy, happy! Happy!
(*Twirls and, stumbling against dais, sprawls back against bed.*)

SHE

Are you all right?

HE

Happy!

SHE

I suddenly feel like saying all sorts of shocking things.

HE

Go on.

SHE

Listen—no, in your ear . . . (SHE *wants to whisper something but is checked by what she sees*) Oh! Michael . . .

HE

(*Faces her*)

What?

SHE

No, don't move. (*Looks at ear again*) Let me see the other one. (HE *turns his head and* SHE *looks at his other ear*) You pig!

HE

What is it?

SHE

Don't you ever wash?

HE

Every day.

SHE

All over?

HE

Oh, well—the main things.

SHE

What *are* the main things?

HE

(*Trying to kiss her*)

My precious . . .

SHE

Your what?

HE

You are my precious. Wouldn't you like to kiss me?

SHE

I would like to go over you from top to bottom, with hot
water and soap; that's what I would like to do.

HE

Please do.

SHE

Oh, well—don't let's dwell on it. (SHE *sits on trunk*) Ouch!

HE

Sweetheart! What's the matter?

SHE

Ouch! My shoes are hurting me. I must take them off or I'll faint.

HE

Let me do it! Please . . . (SHE *puts out her foot.* HE *kneels and tenderly pulls her skirt back and kisses her shoe.*)

SHE

Michael, please, they hurt me so.

HE

(*Kisses her foot again; when* SHE *wants to take shoe off herself*)
No, no, dearest! Let me do it, please let me do it. (HE *takes her shoe again.*)

SHE

But you take such a long time.

HE

(*Untying bow on shoe*)
Isn't that heaven? I could spend the whole night undressing you.

SHE

I didn't ask you to undress me. I only asked you to help me out of my shoes.

HE

I would help you out of anything you ask, dear heart. (*Takes off shoe.*)

SHE

(*Withdraws her foot*)

Now that's one, and now . . . (*As* SHE *leans forward to take off other shoe herself, sees him, still on his knees, leaning back and staring at her*) Please, Michael, don't look at me so creepily. Please get undre . . . Take your hat off!

(HE *takes hat off, puts it on trunk.*)

HE

Agnes, do you remember what I told you when we first met?

SHE

No . . .

HE

That we had met in a former existence.

SHE

Oh, that.

HE

I am absolutely certain of it now.

SHE

Of what?

HE

That moment, just now, I suddenly had the feeling of having experienced all this before.

SHE

Did you really?

HE

You sitting here just as you are, I on my knees in front of you in a hired suit, just before we . . .

SHE

What?

HE

(*Putting shoe down,* HE *leans against her knee*)
Oh, darling, I am happy.

SHE

Must you make me cry?

HE

You should, you know. This is a very sad occasion, really.
Your youth is over.

SHE

(*Pushing him back and getting up*)
I want to go home.

HE

What . . .

SHE

I can't! I want to go home!

HE

(*Still on knees*)
Darling, what's the matter? What have I done?

SHE

(*Picks up shoe*)
I want to go home. I should never have married you.

HE

(*Rises*)
Agnes . . .

SHE

How can you! How dare you say such a thing!

HE

But what . . . I haven't said a thing all night but that I was . . .

SHE

My youth over! That's what you would like! Undressing me, the whole night long, with your hat on and unwashed ears and . . . oh!
(SHE *puts her arms around his neck and weeps.*)

HE

(*Comforting her inexperiencedly*)
That's right, darling; that's it; you cry, my dearest; that's the spirit.

SHE

That's . . . that's why you made me drink such a lot, taking nothing yourself all the time.

HE

Why, I've had at least three bottles.

SHE

Then what did you say? What did you say, when you threw me on the bed?

HE

Threw?

SHE

"If I'm drunk, I'm drunk with happiness." That's what you said.

HE

But, darling, only a minute ago you said yourself . . .

SHE

I did not!

HE

Well, of all the . . . (*Takes her by the shoulders*) Here—smell! (*Breathes at her with his mouth wide open*) Ho, ho, ho!

SHE

(*Escaping the kiss she wants by hiding her face against his shoulder*)
Oh, I'm so dizzy.

HE

I love you.

SHE

I'm so embarrassed.

HE

Why?

SHE

Because I'm so dizzy.

HE

So am I.

SHE

Dizzy?

HE

Embarrassed.

SHE

Why?

HE

Oh, well, you know. It would have been such a relief if I could have spent the whole night taking off your shoes.

SHE

And then have breakfast, straightaway, yes?

HE

Yes. Agnes, I . . . I don't revolt you, do I?

SHE

You? Why on earth should you?

HE

Well, I mean—those ears and . . . things, you know.

SHE

But, darling, I said that only because of other people. What do I care?

HE

And Agnes . . . there's something I should tell you.

SHE

Why tell it just now?

HE

You're right. (*Puts hat on*) I'm such a fool that I . . . (SHE *frowns.* HE *takes hat off again and puts it on trunk*) Would you like something to drink?

SHE

Heavens, no. Don't talk about drinking.

HE

A glass of water, I mean. (*Picks up glass and carafe*) After all that champagne.

SHE

Michael, please talk about something else. I—I really couldn't just now, honestly.

HE

Well, I think I will.
(*Pours glass of water.*)

SHE

Did you write a poem for tonight?

HE

No.

SHE

What a pity! I thought you would have written something beautiful for our wedding.

HE

No.

SHE

Nothing at all?

HE

No.

SHE

You're blushing. Please read it to me.

HE

I haven't got one, darling, really, I haven't.

SHE

You're lying. I can tell by your eyes that you are lying.

HE

As a matter of fact, you wouldn't like it, darling; it's rather modern. There is another one I'm writing just now . . .

SHE

I want to hear the one about our wedding.

HE

Never before in my whole life have I told anybody anything about a poem I hadn't finished . . .

SHE

Is it in your pocket?
(*Starts to pick his pockets.*)

HE
(*Trying to keep her hands back, sits in chair*)
I think it's going to be wonderful. "The Fountain of the Royal Gardens."

SHE
Why may I not hear the one about our wedding?

HE
Darling, don't you think it much more special, just now, something nobody else has ever heard before?

SHE
Has anybody heard the one about our wedding, then?

HE
(*Takes poems from pocket*)
Listen, tell me what you think of the permutation of the consonants, the onomatopoeia, I mean: "Hissing shoots the slender shower; out of shining, slimy stone. . . ."

SHE
No.

HE
"Swaying shivers sparkling flower; rainbow shimmers in the foam." (SHE *starts toward door*) "Flashing, dashing, splashing, crashing . . ." (SHE *hurries to the door, picking up suitcase from chest as she goes*) Where are you going?

SHE
(SHE *opens door, taking the key from the lock*)
Back in a minute.
(*Exits, shuts door, locks it.*)

HE

Why are you taking your suitcase? (*Rises and runs to door;
drops poems on chest as he goes*) Agnes, darling! Agnes!
Agnes! (*Tries to open the locked door.* HE *turns, sees her shoes,
picks them up and smiles. Suddenly, a thought strikes him. He
drops the shoes, runs onto dais, picks up suitcase there, starts to
put it on bed, stops, turns, then puts suitcase on arms of chair.
He opens the case, takes out nightcap and puts it on his head.
He rips off his coat and vest, shirt and tie. As he starts to take
his trousers off, he stops, listens, runs to door, listens again. He
then takes the trousers off. He takes nightshirt from case, goes
to foot of bed, throws nightshirt on bed and sits on chest and
hurriedly takes off his shoes. Then he pauses, looks toward the
door in embarrassment. He quickly puts the shoes back on
again, gets into the nightshirt, pulls his trousers on over it;
then his coat. He moves a few steps, turns, sees his vest, shirt
and tie on trunk where he had thrown them. He tosses them
into the suitcase, fastens it, puts suitcase in wardrobe; starts to
washstand, stops, looks toward door. Then he quickly goes
down to washstand, picks up towel, dampens one corner of it
in pitcher of water and starts to wash his right ear.* SHE *enters.
As* HE *hears door open, he sits in chair and folds his arms.* SHE
*closes the door and puts the key back in the lock. Her dress is
changed somehow; it looks untidier and she has taken off her
wedding hat.* SHE *turns from door, spots him sitting in the
chair, the collar of his jacket upturned and the nightcap on
his head.*)

HE

Hullo.

SHE

What—what are you doing?

HE

Sitting.

SHE

What on earth is that?

HE

What?

SHE

On your head?

HE

Oh . . .

SHE

Do you wear a nightcap?

HE

Oh, no. Just now when there's a draft.
(*Rises, takes cap off and puts it in his pocket.*)

SHE

Is that a nightshirt?

HE

What have you got on?

SHE

My father has been wearing pajamas for ages.

HE

Oh, has he really? Well, I don't.

SHE

Why have you . . . changed?

HE

Why have you?

SHE

I? Oh . . . I'm sleepy.

HE

So am I.

SHE

Well, then, shall we . . .

HE

Why, yes . . . let's.

SHE

All right. Which side do you want?

HE

I? Oh, well. . . . I don't care, really. Any side that suits you
is all right with me.

SHE

I think I would like the far side. Because of the door.

HE

The door?

SHE

(*Turns back quilt*)

Because of breakfast, and in case somebody should knock.
You could answer it.

HE

I see.

SHE

(*Picks up "God Is Love" pillow from bed*)
What's this?

HE

What?

SHE

This little pillow? Did you put that there?

HE

Of course not! What's it got written on it?

SHE

"God Is Love." Oh, how sweet! Mother must have done that.
Wasn't that lovely of her?
(*Puts pillow back on bed.*)

HE

(*Looks at door*)
Yes, lovely.
(SHE *turns away and starts undressing.* HE *takes off his coat.* SHE *turns. After an embarrassing moment in which neither of them can think of anything to say:*)

SHE

Michael, please turn 'round.

HE

Oh, I'm so sorry . . . I didn't realize . . .

(HE *sits down on the edge of the chest, putting his coat beside him, and takes off his shoes and socks.* SHE *steps out of dress and hangs it in wardrobe. Goes back up onto dais.*)

SHE

It's rather a pretty bed, isn't it?

HE

Yes, it is, isn't it? It was my father's, you know.

SHE

Not your mother's?

HE

Yes, of course, my parents'. I was born in it, you know.

SHE

Michael . . .

HE
(*Turning toward her*)
Yes, darling?

SHE
(*Backing up*)
No, don't look! Michael?

HE
(*Turning away*)
Yes?

SHE

Tell me how much you love me, once more.

HE

I can't any more.

SHE

What?

HE

I can't love you any more than I'm doing. I wor . . . I'm the hap . . . I'm mad about you.

SHE

That's what I am about you. Honestly.

HE

That is nice, dear.

SHE

I am so happy, I couldn't be happier.

HE

That is lovely, darling.

SHE

And I wouldn't want to be, either.

HE

What?

SHE

Happier.

HE

I see.

SHE

I wish that everything could stay as it was—before today. I couldn't stand any more—happiness. Could you?

HE

God, no.

SHE

How coldly you say that!

HE

But what the blazing hell do you expect me to say?

SHE

Michael! Is that language for the wedding ni . . . before going to sleep? You ought to be ashamed of yourself!

HE

But damn it, Agnes . . . (*Sneezes*) I—I've got a splitting headache and I'm dying of cold feet. (*Takes nightcap from pocket and puts it on.*)

SHE

(*Takes off her slippers*)
Then why don't you get into bed, silly? (HE *rises*) No! A moment! A moment! (HE *turns away.* SHE *gets into bed, the "God Is Love" pillow beneath her head.* HE *stands for a moment in embarrassment, starts to take off his trousers, then realizing that the room is still brightly lit, he goes to bracket, right of arch, and turns it off.*)

HE

May I turn 'round now?

SHE

Yes.

(HE *reaches to turn down the bracket but is stopped by her interruption.*)

SHE

Wait! It can't leak, can it? The lamp, I mean?

HE

Of course not.

SHE

But I think I smell gas.

HE

(*Reaches behind him and takes her hand*)
Darling, listen. You are an angel, and I'm madly in love with you, and I'm embarrassed to death and so are you, and that's the reason why we . . . Good night.
(HE *reaches up and turns down the bracket.*)

SHE

Good night. (HE *takes off his trousers and puts them on chair*) Can you find your way?

HE

Yes, yes . . . (*Going back up to bed, stubs his toe*) Ouch!

SHE

Michael! What are you doing?

HE
(On dais)

Nothing. I hurt my toe.
    (HE *gets into bed.*)

SHE

Oh, I'm so sorry. *(Long silence)* Do get into bed carefully, won't you?

HE

I'm in it already.

SHE
(After another silence)

Michael?

HE

Yes?

SHE

Michael, what was it you didn't want to tell me tonight?

HE

Ah . . .

SHE

You may tell me now, if you like. I'm not embarrassed any more, somehow.

HE

Well . . .

SHE

If you tell me what it was, I'll tell you something as well.

HE

What?

SHE

But you must tell me as well. Promise me.

HE

Yes.

SHE

No, promise me first.

HE

All right. I promise.

SHE

I . . . I've never seen a man . . . before . . . completely.
Never.

HE

Oh, well—you haven't missed much.

SHE

And you?

HE

Oh.

SHE

Have you ever seen a woman before . . . completely?

HE

Well . . .

SHE

What does that mean?

HE

You know, I once had my fortune told by a gypsy.

SHE

Oh . . .

HE

She said I'd have a very happy married life, that I'd live to a ripe old age, and she said that everything would turn out all right.

SHE

And was she . . . naked?

HE

Of course not! She went from house to house with a goat.

SHE

Oh . . . Good night.

HE

Good night. (*Pause*) Are you comfy?

SHE

Oh, yes.

HE

Not too cold?

SHE

Heavens, no. I'm simply boiling. And you?

HE

Rather cold, really.

SHE
(*After a silence*)

Michael!

HE

Yes?

SHE

Michael! Now I'm sure that I smell gas.
(SHE *sits up.*)

HE

That must be the drink.

SHE

Do you still smell of drink that much? I can't believe it.

HE

Yes.

SHE

Let me smell your breath again.

HE

Oh, please, Agnes, let's try to go to sleep.

SHE

No, Michael, I want to smell it. If it is the gas, we may be dead tomorrow, both of us.

HE

Oh, well . . .

SHE

Oh, well! Do you want to die?

HE

Sometimes.

SHE

Now?

HE

No, no.

SHE

Please, Michael, let me have a little sniff before I go to sleep; otherwise, I won't close an eye. (*Lies down*) Please, Michael.

HE
(*Sits up and leans over her*)
Ho! Ho! Ho! (*Lies back on his pillow*) There.

SHE
(*Sits up and leans over him*)
I don't smell a thing. Do it again.

HB

Ho! Ho!

SHE

Again?

HE

Ho, ho.

SHE

Again . . .

Curtain

ACT ONE

SCENE II

1891. Late Afternoon.

The same bedroom. To the right, a cradle.
HE *is lying in the fourposter, with a towel wrapped around his head. The bed is strewn with books, papers, an oversized dinner bell and his dressing gown. Heaps of books and papers are on the dais at foot of bed.*
When the curtain rises, HE *awakens.*

HE
(*From beneath the blankets*)
Agnes! Agnes! (*Sits up*) Agnes!
(*Picks up bell and rings loudly and insistently.*)

SHE
(*Enters hurriedly carrying a pile of clean laundry.*
SHE *is very pregnant*)
Yes, yes, yes, yes, yes. What is it?

HE
I've got such a pain! (SHE *returns to door and closes it*)
I can't stand it any longer!

SHE
(*Putting laundry on chest*)
Now, come, come, darling. Don't dramatize. I'll soak your towel again.

31

HE

No! It isn't my head. It's shifted to here.
(*Puts his hand on his back.*)

SHE

Where?

HE

Here! (*Leans forward. Places her hand on the painful
spot*) Here! What is there? Do you feel anything?

SHE

You've got a pain there?

HE

As if I'd been stabbed. No, don't take your hand away . . .
Oh, that's nice.

SHE

(*Suspiciously*)
But what sort of pain? Does it come in—in waves? First
almost nothing and then growing until you could scream?

HE

That's right. How do you know . . .

SHE

Micky, that's impossible.

HE

What's impossible? Do you think I'm shamming?

SHE

You're having labor pains!

HE

You're crazy!

SHE

And all the time . . . all the time I've put up a brave front because I thought you were really ill!

HE

But I *am* ill! What do you think? That I lay here groaning and sweating just for the fun of it?

SHE

All the time I've been thinking of *you!*

HE

I've done nothing else, day and night, but think of *you!* How else do you think I got the pains *you're* supposed to have? (SHE *sobs*) Oh, hell! This is driving me mad!
    (HE *jumps out of bed.*)

SHE

Micky! (HE *tears open the wardrobe*) Micky, what are you doing?

HE

Where are my shoes?

SHE

Michael! You aren't running away, are you?

HE

(*Gets clothes from wardrobe*)
I'm going to get that doctor.

SHE
(*Rises*)
No, Michael, you mustn't.

HE
(*Puts clothes on chair*)
If I drop dead on the pavement, I'm going to get that doctor! I'm not going to leave you in this condition a minute longer. He said so himself, the moment you got those pains . . .

(*Kneels, looks under bed.*)

SHE
When *I* got them! Not when *you* got them!

HE
Don't you feel anything?

SHE
Nothing! Nothing at all.

HE
Then I don't understand why you were crying just now.

SHE
Please, darling, please go back to bed. You'll catch a cold with those bare feet and you're perspiring so freely. Please, darling.

HE
But I don't want to.

SHE
(*Pops him into bed*)
I want you to. Uppy-pie, in you go!

HE

Anyone would think you wanted me to be ill.

SHE

No grumbling, no growling. (*Puts "God Is Love" pillow behind his head*) There! Comfy?
  (*Goes to chest.*)

HE

No! (HE *throws pillow to floor.*) I'm scared.

SHE

What on earth of?

HE

Of—of the baby. Aren't you?

SHE

Good Heavens, no. Why should I? It's the most natural thing in the world, isn't it? And I'm feeling all right.
  (*Picks up sewing.*)

HE

You have changed a lot, do you know that?

SHE
(*Starts sewing*)

Since when?

HE

Since you became a mother.

SHE

But I'm not a mother yet.

SHE

Then you don't realize it yourself. Suddenly you have become a woman.

SHE

Have I ever been anything else?

HE

A silly child.

SHE

So that's what you thought of me when we married?

HE

When we married, my feet were off the ground.

SHE

Well, you've changed a lot, too.

HE

Of course I have. I have become a man.

SHE

Hah!

HE

Well, haven't I? Aren't I much more calm, composed . . .

SHE

(*Picks up rattle from bassinette and throws it to him*)
You're a baby!

HE

(*Throws covers back and sits on edge of bed*)

That's right! Humiliate me! Lose no opportunity of re-
minding me that I'm the male animal that's done its duty
and now can be dismissed!

(*Jumps out.*)

SHE

Michael!

HE

Yes! A drone, that's what I am! The one thing lacking is
that you should devour me. The bees . . .

SHE

Michael, Michael, what's the matter?

(*Reaches out to him.*)

HE

I'm afraid!

SHE

But I'm not, Michael, honestly, not a bit.

HE

I'm afraid of something else.

SHE

What?

HE

That I've lost you.

SHE
(*Rises, goes to him*)
Michael, look at me . . . What did the doctor tell you?

HE
It's got nothing to do with the doctor. It's got nothing to do with you either. It's got to do with me.

SHE
(*Puts arms about him*)
But you're going to be all right, aren't you?

HE
(*Breaks away*)
I'd never be all right again, if I've lost you.

SHE
What are you talking about? You've got me right here, haven't you?

HE
But your heart, that's gone. I wish I was lying in that cradle.

SHE
(*Puts her arms around him again*)
You fool . . . (*Kisses him*) You can't be as stupid as all that. No, Michael.

HE
Listen! Before that cuckoo pushes me out of the nest, I want to tell you once more that I love you. Love you, just as you are . . . I thought I loved you when I married you, but that wasn't you at all. That was a romantic illusion. I loved a sort of fairy princess with a doll's smile and a . . . well, anyway not a princess with hiccoughs and cold feet, scratching her stomach in her sleep . . .

SHE

Michael!

HE

(*Takes her hand*) I thought I was marrying a princess and I woke up to find a friend, a wife . . . You know, sometimes when I lay awake longer than you, with my arm around your shoulder and your head on my chest, I thought with pity of all those lonely men staring at the ceiling or writing poems . . . pity, and such happiness that I knew at that very moment it wouldn't last. I was right, that's all.

SHE

Well, if you thought about a princess, I thought about a poet.

HE

Oh?

SHE

You didn't know that I had cold feet, and every now and again I get an attack of hiccoughs . .

HE

You don't do anything else the whole night long.

SHE

What?

HE

Scratch your stomach and sniff and snort and smack your lips, but go on.

SHE

And you lie listening to all this without waking me up?

HE

Yes. Because I don't know anything in the world I'd rather listen to. (*Kisses her*) Got anything to say to that?

SHE

Yes, but I won't say it.

HE

Why not?

SHE

Never mind, darling, you stay just as you are.

HE

Miserable, deserted, alone? You do nothing else all day and night but fuss over that child—eight months now! First it was knitting panties, then sewing dresses, fitting out the layette, rigging the cradle . . .

SHE

And all this time you sat quietly in your corner, didn't you?

HE

I retired into the background as becomes a man who recognizes that he is one too many.

SHE

(*Rises, goes to him*)
Oh, angel! (*Puts her arms around his neck and kisses him*) Do you still not understand why I love you so much?

HE

You . . . you noticed how I blotted myself out?

SHE

Did I!

HE

I didn't think you did.

SHE

You helped me more than all model husbands put together. Without you I would have been frightened to death for eight whole months. But now I simply had no time.

HE

I believe you're teasing me.

SHE

I love you. Do you believe that?

HE

Of course.

SHE

Must I prove it to you?

HE

Oh, no. I'm perfectly prepared to take your word for it.

SHE

All right, if you like, we'll send the child to a home.

HE

What?

SHE

And then we'll go and look at it every Sunday.

HE

Agnes, why do you tease me?

SHE

Darling, I'm not teasing you. I'm telling you the truth. Even if I were going to have twenty children, you are my husband and I'd rather leave them as foundlings . . .
>   (SHE *grasps at her back and turns.* HE *stares at her in horror.*)

HE

Darling, what—what is it? Agnes!

SHE
>   (*Clutching the bed post*)

Oh!

HE
>   (*Picks up clothes, goes to her*)

The doctor! For God's sake, the doctor!

SHE

No . . . oh, oh! Don't . . . not the doctor. Stay here.

HE

Darling, darling! Angel! Agnes, my love! What must I do? For God's sake, I must do something!

SHE
>   (*Sings, convulsed by pain, loudly*)

"Yankee Doodle went to town,
Riding on a pony . . ."

HE

Agnes!

SHE

(*Sings on*)

"He stuck a feather in his hat,
And called it macaroni."

HE

(*Takes her by shoulders*)

Agnes!

SHE

Oh, Micky . . . What are you doing?

HE

I—I thought you were going mad.

SHE

I? Why?

HE

(*Seats her on chest*)

You started to sing.

SHE

(*Sitting*)

Oh, yes. The doctor said if those pains started, I had to sing. That would help. I must have done it automatically.

HE

Are you all right now?

SHE

Oh, yes, yes.

HE

Now you just sit here quietly. I'll get the doctor.

SHE

No, Michael, you mustn't. He said we weren't to bother him until the pains came regularly.

HE

Regularly? But I won't be a minute.
(*Picks up clothes.*)

SHE

Oh, please, please don't go away. Oh, I wish Mother were here.

HE

(*Puts clothes on bed*)
Now, don't worry! This is the most natural thing in the world. You just sit here quietly. I'll put some clothes on and . . .

SHE

Oh, no, no Micky, please, please don't fuss. I wish it didn't have to happen so soon.

HE

(*Turns upstage with back to audience, takes off
pajama pants. Puts on trousers*)
Yes.

SHE

(*Picks up pajama pants*)
I'm not nearly ready for it yet . . .

HE

(*Taking off robe and putting it on bed*)
Well, I am. Honestly, I am. I can't wait to—to go fishing

with him, if it's a boy, and—and, if it's a girl, go for walks, nature rambles. . . .

(*Goes to wardrobe and gets tie.*)

SHE

But that won't happen for years. First, there will be years of crying and diapers and bottles . . .

HE

(*Ties tie*)

I don't mind, darling. Honestly, I don't. I'll—find something to do. I'll work and—and go fishing alone. You're never going to have to worry about . . .

SHE

(*In pain again*)

Oh!

HE

(*Goes to her, kneels*)

Another one?

SHE

No. No, I don't think so.

HE

Now, why don't you go to bed? (*Throws robe and coat on chest. Fixes bed linen*) You go to bed. I'll finish dressing and make you a nice cup of tea, yes?

SHE

No, no, thank you, darling. I think I'll stay right where I am. Oh, I haven't done nearly all the things I should have done. There's still half the laundry out on the roof and . . .

HE
(*Stops her*)
Agnes, do stop worrying. As soon as I've finished dressing,
I'll go to the roof and take the washing in for you.
(*Seats her on chest.*)

SHE
(*Puts arms about his waist*)
No, please don't leave me alone.

HE
(*Puts his arms about her shoulders*)
All right, all right. There's nothing to be afraid of. This
has been going on for millions and millions of years. Now
what would you like? Shall I read you something? (*Goes
to the bed. Picks up books*) Schopenhauer, *Alice in Wonder-
land*?

SHE
No.

HE
I know. I've started a new book. It's only half a page. Shall
I read you that? Yes?
(*He picks up writing pad.*)

SHE
(*Biting her lip*)
Yes . . .

HE
(*Sits on foot of bed*)
It's going to be a trilogy. It's called "Burnt Corn, the Story
of a Rural Love." Do you like that as a title?

SHE
(*Biting her lips*)
I think that's wonderful.

HE
Now this is how it opens . . . (*Takes hold of her hand*)
Are you all right?

SHE
Fine.

HE
(*Reads*)
"When she entered the attic with the double bed, she bent
her head, partly out of reverence for the temple where she had
worshipped and sacrificed, partly because the ceiling was so
low. It was not the first time she had returned to that
shrine . . ." (SHE *has a pain*) Are you all right?

SHE
Oh, Micky, I love you so. Don't, don't let's ever . . .
(SHE *has another pain.* HE *drops pad and kneels before
her.*)

SHE
(SHE *buries her head in his shoulder, then looks up*)
Now . . . now, I think you'd better go and call him.

HE
I will, my darling. (*Puts on his coat. Goes to door, stops,
returns to her*) Now, you just sit tight.
(*Goes to door, returns and kisses her. Goes back to
door, turns, sees bassinette, runs to it and pulls it over
close to her and exits.*)

Curtain

ACT TWO

ACT TWO

SCENE I

1901. Night.

*The same room, ten years later. The only piece of furniture
left from the preceding scene is the fourposter, but it has been
fitted out with new brocade curtains. Paintings hang on the
walls; expensive furniture crowds the room. No washstand
any more, but a bathroom to the left. Where the wardrobe
stood in the preceding act, the wall has been removed and this
has become an entrance to a dressing room. The whole thing
is very costly, very grand and very new. Only one side of the
bed has been made; there is only one pillow on the bed with
the "God Is Love" pillow on top of it.*

AT RISE, there is no one in the room. SHE *enters and slams
the door behind her.* SHE *stands at the foot of the bed, remov-
ing her evening gloves. Goes to dressing table, throws gloves
on the table, and is stopped by a knock at the door.* SHE
stands for a moment. The knock is repeated, more insistently.

SHE
(*After a pause*)
Come in.

HE
(*Enters, closes door*)
Excuse me. (*Goes to the dressing room, gets his night
clothes, re-enters and crosses to door*) Good night.

51

SHE

(*As* HE *opens door*)

You certainly were the life and soul of the party this evening, with your interminable little stories.

HE

(*Starts out, stops, turns*)

My dear, if you don't enjoy playing second fiddle, I suggest
you either quit the orchestra or form one of your own.
(*Goes out and shuts door.*)

SHE

(*Mutters after a moment's stupefaction*)

Now, I've had enough! (*Runs to door, rips it open, stands
in hallway and calls off*) Michael! (*Then bellows*) Michael!
Come here!

HE

(*Pops in. Has top hat and cane in hand
and evening cape over arm*)

Have you taken leave of your senses? The servants . . .

SHE

I don't care if the whole town hears it. (HE *exits*) Come
back, I say!

HE

(*Re-enters*)

All right. This situation is no longer bearable!
(*Closes door.*)

SHE

What on earth is the matter with you?

HE

Now, let me tell you one thing, calmly. (SHE *goes to dressing table, takes off plume, throws it on table*) My greatest mistake has been to play up to you, plying you with presents . . .

SHE

I like that!
(*Picks up gloves.*)

HE

Calmly! Do you know what I should have done? I should have packed you off to boarding school, big as you are, to learn deportment.

SHE

Deportment for what?

HE

To be worthy of *me*.

SHE

The pompous ass whose book sold three hundred thousand copies!

HE

That is entirely beside the point.

SHE

It is right to the point! Before you had written that cursed novel, the rest of the world helped me to keep you sane. Every time you had finished a book or a play or God knows what, and considered yourself to be the greatest genius since

Shakespeare . . . (HE *says, "Now really!"*) I was frightened to death that it might turn out to be a success. But, thank Heaven, it turned out to be such a thorough failure every time, that I won the battle with your megalomania. But now, now this book, the only book you ever confessed to be trash until you read the papers . . . Oh, what's the use!

HE

My dear woman, I may be vain, but you are making a tragic mistake.

SHE

(*Laughs*)

Now listen! Just listen to him! To be married to a man for eleven years, and then to be addressed like a public meeting. Tragic mistake! Can't you hear yourself, you poor darling idiot, that you've sold your soul to a sentimental novel?

HE

Agnes, are you going on like this, or must I . . .

SHE

Yes, yes, you must! You *shall* hear it. (HE *pounds floor with evening cane*) And don't interrupt me! There is only one person in this world who loves you in spite of what you are, and let me tell you . . .

HE

You are mistaken. There is a person in this world who loves me—because of what I am.

SHE

And what are you, my darling?

HE

Ask her.

SHE

Her . . .

HE

Yes.

SHE

Oh . . . (*Holds onto bed post*) Who is she?

HE

You don't know her.

SHE

Is she . . . young? How young?

HE

No. I'll be damned if I go on with this. You look like a corpse.

SHE

A corpse?

HE

So pale, I mean. (*At door*) Agnes, I'm not such a monster, that . . . Sit down. Please, Agnes, do sit . . . Agnes!

SHE

(*Turns away.*)

No, no . . . it's nothing. I'm all right. What do you think? That I should faint in my thirty-first year because of something so . . . so ordinary?

HE

Ordinary?

SHE

With two children? I didn't faint when Robert had the mumps, did I?

HE

Don't you think this is a little different?

SHE

No, Michael. This belongs to the family medicine chest.

HE

I love her!

SHE

So, not me any more? (HE *doesn't reply*) I don't mean as a friend, or as . . . as the mother of your children, but as a wife? You may tell me honestly, really. Is that why you've been sleeping in the study?

HE

I haven't slept a wink.

SHE

I see. It must be Cook who snores.

HE

Since when do I snore?

SHE

Not you, dear, Cook. Every night when I went down the passage.

HE

(*Goes to the door, opens it*)

Good night!

SHE

Sleep well.

HE

What was that?

SHE

Sleep well.

HE

Oh . . . (*Stops at door, then slams it shut*) No! I'll be damned, I won't stand it!

SHE

What is the matter?

HE

Cook snores! Agnes, I love somebody else! It's driving me crazy! You, the children, she, the children, you . . . for three weeks I have lived through hell, and all you've got to say is "Cook snores!"

SHE

But, darling . . .

HE

No, no, no, no! You are so damned sure of yourself that it makes me sick! I know you don't take this seriously, but believe me, I love that woman! I must have that woman or I'll go mad!

SHE

Haven't you . . . had her yet?

HE

At last! Thank God, a sign of life. Why haven't you looked at me like that before? I have begged, implored, crawled to you for a little understanding and warmth, and love, and got nothing. Even my book, that was inspired by you, longing for you—right from the beginning you have seen it as a rival. Whatever I did, whatever I tried: a carriage, servants, money, dresses, paintings, everything . . . you hated that book. And now? Now you have driven me into somebody else's arms. Somebody else, who understands at least one thing clearly: that she will have to share me with my work.

SHE

Does she understand that she will have to share you with other women as well?

HE

She doesn't need to. At last I have found a woman who'll live with my work, and a better guarantee of my faithfulness nobody could have.

SHE

But how does she live with it? What does she do?

HE

She listens. She encourages me—with a look, a touch, a—well, an encouragement. When I cheer, she cheers with me, when I meditate, she meditates with me . . .

SHE

And when you throw crockery, she throws crockery with you?

HE

Haven't you understood one single word of what I have been saying? Won't you, can't you see that I have changed?

SHE

No.

HE

Then you are blind! That's all I can say. At any rate, *you've* changed.

SHE

I!

HE

No, don't let's start that.

SHE

Go on.

HE

No, it's senseless. No reason to torture you any longer, once
I have . . .

SHE

Once you have tasted blood.

HE

I . . . I'm sorry it was necessary for me to hurt you. It
couldn't very well have been done otherwise. I'm at the mercy
of a feeling stronger than I.

SHE

Rotten, isn't it?

HE

Horrible.

SHE

And yet . . . at the same time not altogether.

HE

No. On the other hand, it's delicious.

SHE

The greatest thing a human being can experience.

HE

I'm glad you understand it so well.

SHE

Understand? Why, of course. It's human isn't it?

HE

How do you come to know that?

SHE

What?

HE

That it's—human?

SHE

Well, I'm a human being, aren't I?

HE

I never heard you talk like this before. What's the matter
with you?

SHE

Well, I might have my experiences too, mightn't I? Good
night.

HE

Just a minute! I want to hear a little more about this!

SHE

But I know it now, dear.

HE

Yes, you do! But I don't! What sort of experiences are you
referring to?

SHE

Now, listen, my little friend! You have dismissed me without notice, and I haven't complained once as any other house-
keeper would have done. I have accepted the facts because I
know a human being is at the mercy of this feeling, however
horrible and at the same time delicious it may be.

HE

Agnes!

SHE

I really don't understand you. I am not thwarting you in the least, and instead of your going away happily and relieved that you are not leaving a helpless wreck behind . . .

HE

You might answer just one plain question before . . . we finish this business. Have you . . . aren't you going to be alone, if I leave you?

SHE

Alone? I've got the children, haven't I?

HE

That's not at all certain.

SHE

(*After a shaky silence*)

You had better leave this room very quickly now, before you get to know a side of me that might surprise you a lot.

HE

I have, I'm afraid. I demand an answer. Have you a lover?

SHE

(*Goes to door, opens it*)

Good night.

HE

For eleven long years I have believed in you! You were the purest, the . . .

SHE

(*Interrupting*)

The noblest thing in my life! Good night!

HE

If you don't answer my question, you'll never see me again.

SHE

Get out of here!

HE

No.

SHE

All right. Then there's only one thing left to be done.
(*She picks up wrap from bed and exits into dressing room.*)

HE

What? What did you want to say? (SHE *does not answer.* SHE *returns with second wrap and overnight case; puts them both on chair and opens case*) What's the meaning of that? (SHE *picks up nightgown and negligee, packs them in case*) Darling, believe me, I won't blame you for anything, only tell me—where are you going?

SHE

(*Goes to dressing table and gets brushes and comb*)
Would you mind calling a cab for me?

HE

Agnes!

SHE

(Packs brushes and comb in case)

Please, Michael, I can't arrive there too late. It is such an embarrassing time already. Pass me my alarm clock, will you?

HE

No, I can't have been mistaken about you that much! Only yesterday you said that I had qualities . . .

SHE

Excuse me.

(Passes him, gets her alarm clock, puts clock in case.)

HE

(Wants to stop her when she passes, but checks himself)

All right. It *is* a solution, anyhow.

SHE

(Closes overnight case, picks it up, puts wrap over arm, goes around chair to him and puts out her hand)

Good-bye, Michael. (HE *blocks her way.*)

HE

Do you really think I'm going to let you do this? Do you?

SHE

A gentleman does not use force when a lady wishes to leave the room.

HE

Oh, I'm so sorry.

(Steps aside.)

SHE

Thank you. (HE *grabs her arm and pulls her back.* SHE *drops her suitcase and wrap in the struggle;* HE *flings her up onto the bed*) Michael! Let me go! Let me go! I . . .

HE

Now look, I've put up with all the nonsense from you . . . (SHE *succeeds in tearing herself free, gets off the bed and kicks his shin*) Ouch! (HE *grasps at his shinbone and limps, leans against arm of sofa.*)

SHE

Get out!

HE

Right on my scar!

SHE

Get out! (HE *takes off his coat, throws it on chair. As* HE *starts toward her:*) I'll scream the house down if you dare come near me! (SHE *scrambles back up onto bed.*)

HE

Where's my pillow?

SHE

(*Reaching for bell pull*)
Get out or I'll ring the bell!

HE

(*As he exits to dressing room*)
Make up that bed properly.

SHE

You're the vilest swine God ever created!

HE

(*Re-enters carrying pillow*)

If I have to make you hoarse and broken for the rest of your life, you'll know that I am a man. Make up that bed!

(*Throws pillow at her.*)

SHE

I would rather . . .

HE

And shut up! Get off there!

SHE

(*Strikes at him with "God Is Love" pillow*)

You are the silliest hack-writer I ever . . .

HE

(*Grabs "God Is Love" pillow and throws it*)

Get off, or I'll drag you off!

SHE

(*Gets off bed*)

And that book of yours is rubbish.

HE

What did I tell you after I finished it? Listening to me once in awhile wouldn't do you any harm. Here! (*Throws comforter at her*) Fold that!

SHE

(*Throws it back*)

Fold it yourself!

HE

(Throws it back)

Fold it!

> (SHE *goes at him and* HE *grasps her hands.* SHE *still tries to flail him.* HE *slips in the struggle and sits on dais.* SHE *tries to pound his head.* HE *regains his feet and pinions her arms behind her.)*

SHE

(As HE *grasps her face with left hand)*

I'll bite you!

HE

If you could see your eyes now, you'd close them. They're blinding.

SHE

With hatred!

HE

With love.

> *(Gives her a quick kiss;* SHE *breaks free.* HE *gets on guard.)*

SHE

> *(Looks at him speechless for a moment, then sits on the bed, away from him, sobbing)*

I wish I were dead. I want to be dead, dead . . .

HE

> *(Sits on edge of bed, holding shin)*

Before you die, look in my eyes, just once. Look! *(Turns her to him.* SHE *looks)* What do you see there?

SHE

Wrinkles!

HE

(*Picks up evening pumps which have come off in the scuffle and goes back onto dais*)
That's how long it is since you last looked. (*Sits on bed and puts one pump on*) What else?

SHE

But . . . what about her?

HE

I was lonely.

SHE

(*Stands*)

You'd better go now.

HE

Weren't you?

SHE

Please go.

HE

(*Picks up evening coat.* SHE *picks up his pillow and puts it on chair. At archway, as* HE *puts on other pump:*)
I've started writing a new book.

SHE

When?

HE

A couple of weeks ago.

SHE

And you haven't read me anything yet? Impossible.

HE

I read it to her.

SHE

Oh . . . and?

HE

She liked it all right. But she thought it a little . . . well, coarse.

SHE

You, coarse? What kind of sheep is she?

HE

Shall I go and get the manuscript?

SHE

(*Picks up his pillow*)

Tomorrow.

HE

(*Moves quickly to door and puts hand on door knob*)
No, now!

SHE

(*Goes onto dais, puts his pillow on bed*)
Please . . . tomorrow.

(HE *throws coat onto bench at foot of bed and goes around onto dais and embraces her.*)

Curtain

ACT TWO

Scene II

1908. 4:00 A.M. to dawn.

When the curtain rises, the stage is dark. The door is opened brusquely and HE *enters, wearing an overcoat over his pajamas.* HE *is carrying a bourbon bottle and riding crop.* SHE *is asleep in the fourposter.*

HE
(As HE *enters)*
Agnes! *(Goes to dressing table right of arch and turns on dressing-table lamps)* Agnes, Agnes, look at this!
(Turns on bed-table lamp. HE *shows her brown bourbon bottle.)*

SHE
(Waking up and shielding her eyes with arm)
Huh? What's the matter?

HE
In his drawer, behind a pile of junk—this!

SHE
What?

HE
He's seventeen—eighteen! And it's four o'clock in the morning! And—and now, this!

70

SHE
(Sitting up)

What, for Heaven's sake?

HE
(Hands her the bottle)

Look!

SHE
(Takes bottle and looks at it)

Bourbon!

HE

Your son. The result of your modern upbringing.

SHE

But what—where . . . *(Puts bottle down on bed)* What does all this mean? What's the time?
(Leans over and picks up clock.)

HE
(As HE exits into bathroom)

It's time I took over his education.

SHE

But he told you he would be late tonight. He specially asked permission to go to that dance. I gave him the key myself!

HE
(Re-enters and exits again into dressing room)

Where did you put that thing?

SHE

What thing?

HE

My old shaving strop.

SHE

What do you want that for? (*Lying back in bed*) Come
back to bed.

HE
(*Re-enters*)

So you approve of all this? You think it's perfectly natural
that a child boozes in his bedroom and paints the town until
four o'clock in the morning?

SHE

But, darling, he told you! And surely the child has a right
to a bit of gaiety.

HE

One day let me explain the difference between gaiety and
delirium tremens!

SHE

What are you going to do, Michael?

HE
(*Turns round in the doorway*)

I am going downstairs where I have been since one o'clock
this morning. And when he comes home, I . . .

SHE
(*Climbs out of bed. Picks up robe*)

I won't let you! If you are going to beat that child, you will
have to do so over my dead body!

HE

Don't interfere, Agnes.

SHE

I mean it, Michael! Whatever happens, even if he has taken to opium, I will not let you beat that child!

HE

All right. In that case, we had better call the police.

SHE

But you knew he was coming in late! These children's parties go on till dawn!

HE

(*With a politician's gesture of despair*)
Now, in my young days, if I was told to be in at a certain hour—(*Turns to her for the beginning of a big speech*) I— (*Sees her for the first time*) What in the name of sanity have you got on your head?

SHE

Now, now, that's the very latest thing—everyone's wearing them—

HE

But what *is* it?

SHE

A slumber helmet.

HE

Slumber helmet! Bourbon in the bedroom, children's parties that go on till dawn and slumber helmets. All right. (*Throws*

riding crop on bench at foot of bed and rips off overcoat)
I am going to bed.

SHE

Listen to me, will you?

HE
(*Steps out of slippers*)
I have the choice between bed and the madhouse. I prefer
bed. I have a life to live. Good night! (HE *gets into bed and
pulls the blanket up.* SHE *goes above sofa.* HE *sits up*) I hope
you enjoy being a drunkard's mother!
(*Lies back.*)

SHE

I don't want to spoil your performance as an irate father, but
I can't help thinking what your attitude would be if it were
not Robert, but Lizzie who stayed out late.

HE
(*Sits up*)
Exactly the same! With this difference, that Lizzie would
never do such a thing.

SHE

Ha!

HE

Because she happens to be the only sane member of this
family, except me.
(*Lies back.*)

SHE
(*At arch*)
I could tell you something about her that would . . . No, I'd
better not.

HE

(*Sits up*)

If you think that I am going to fall for that stone-age woman's trick of hinting at something and then stopping . . . That child is as straight and as sensible as—as a glass of milk.

(*Lies back.*)

SHE

Milk!

HE

(*Finds bottle in bed, sits up, puts bottle on bed table, lies back*)

At least she doesn't go to bed with a bottle of bourbon.

SHE

Mmm.

HE

(*Sitting up*)

What—Mmm?

SHE

Nothing, nothing.

HE

Agnes, you aren't by any chance suggesting that she goes to bed with anything else, are you?

SHE

I am not suggesting anything. I am just sick and tired of your coming down like a ton of bricks on that poor boy every time, while she is allowed to do whatever she pleases.

HE

So! I have an unhealthy preference for my daughter. Is that
it?

SHE

I am not saying that. I . . .

HE

All right, say it! Say it!

SHE

What?

HE

Oedipus!

SHE

Who?

HE

Oh! Leave me alone.
(*Under the blankets again.*)

SHE

In his drawer, did you say?

HE

Shut up.

SHE

Darling, I know you never concern yourself with the children's education except for an occasional bout of fatherly hys-
teria, but I think that this time you are going a little too far,
if you don't mind my saying so.

HE

What else do you want me to do? I have to spend every
waking hour earning money. You are my second in command.

I have to leave certain things to you; but if I see that they are obviously going wrong, it is my duty to intervene.

SHE

If that is your conception of our relationship, then you ought to think of something better than a shaving crop and a riding strop.

HE

Riding crop! And it's not a matter of thinking of something better, it's . . .
    (HE *stops because she has suddenly got up and gone to the window, as if she heard something.*)

SHE

Michael!

HE

Is that him?
    (*As* SHE *does not answer,* HE *gets out of bed and grabs his overcoat.*)

SHE

(*Peeking out the window*)
I thought I heard the gate.

HE

(*From the doorway*)
Robert! (*Exits and calls offstage*) Is that you, Robert? (*No answer, so he comes back*) No.

SHE

(*Sits at dressing table, opens powder box*)
Why don't you go back to bed?

HE

Because I'm worried.

SHE

(*Picking up hand mirror and puff and powdering her face*)
Why, that's nonsense!

HE

And so are you.

SHE

What on earth gives you that idea?

HE

That you are powdering your face at four o'clock in the
morning.

SHE

(*Puts down mirror, puff. Realizes that there is no use pretend-
ing any longer, goes to the bottle and picks it up from bed
table*)
What drawer was it?

HE

The one where he keeps all his junk.

SHE

I can't believe it. It can't be true.

HE

Well, there you are.

SHE

How did you find it?

HE

I was sitting downstairs waiting. I got more and more worried
so I decided to go up to his room and see whether perhaps
he had climbed in through the window, and then I happened
to glance into an open drawer, and there it was.

SHE

But it isn't possible. A child can't be drinking on the sly
without his mother knowing it.

HE

We'll have to face it, my dear. He is no longer a child.
When I looked into that drawer and found his old teddy bears,
his steam engine, and then that bottle, I—I can't tell you what
I felt.

SHE

Suppose—of course it isn't—but suppose—it is true, whatever shall we do?

HE

I don't know—see a doctor.

SHE

Nonsense. It's perfectly natural childish curiosity. A boy has
to try everything once.

HE

If that's going to be your attitude, he'll end by trying mur-
der once. By the way, what were you going to say about
Lizzie?

SHE
(Smiles)

She is in love.

HE

What?

SHE

She's secretly engaged.

HE

To whom?

SHE

To the boy next door.

HE

To that—ape? To that pie face?

SHE

I think it's quite serious.

HE

The child is only . . . nonsense!

SHE

She is not a child any more. She's . . . well, the same thing Robert is, I suppose. I wouldn't be surprised if one of these days the boy came to see you to ask for her hand.

HE

If he does, I'll shoot him.

SHE

But, darling . . .

HE

But she's only sixteen! Agnes, this is a nightmare!

SHE

But, sweetheart . . .

HE

She can't be in love, and certainly not with *that!*

SHE

Why not?

HE

After spending her whole life with me, she can't fall in love with something hatched out of an egg.

SHE

Are you suggesting that the only person the child will be allowed to fall in love with is a younger edition of yourself?

HE

Of course not. Don't be indecent. What I mean is that at least we should have given them taste! They should have inherited our taste!

SHE

Well, he seems to have inherited a taste for bourbon.

HE

I don't understand how you can joke about it. This happens to be the worst night of my life.

SHE

I'm not joking, darling I just don't think that there's much point in us sitting up all night worrying ourselves sick about something we obviously can't do anything about until the morning. Come, go back to bed.

HE

You go to bed . . . I'll wait up for him.

SHE

Shall I make you a cup of tea?

HE

Tea! Do you know that we haven't had a single crisis in our life yet for which your ultimate solution wasn't a cup of tea?

SHE

I'm sorry. I was only trying to be sensible about it.

HE

I know you are. I apologize if I've said things that I didn't mean. (*Picks up the bourbon bottle and uncorks it with his left hand.*) I think what we both need is a swig of this. Have we got any glasses up here?

SHE

Only tooth-glasses. (HE *takes a swig, then with a horrified expression thrusts the bottle and cork into her hands and runs to the bathroom.*) Michael!
(SHE *smells the bottle, grimaces.*)

HE

(*Rushing out of bathroom with a nauseated look on his face.*) What is that?

SHE

Cod liver oil!

HE

Oh!

(*Runs back into bathroom.*)

SHE

(*Takes handkerchief from pocket, wipes bottle*)
How on earth did it get into this bottle?

HE

God knows! (*Re-enters to just outside bathroom door.* HE
carries a glass of water) I think that little monster must have
been trying to set a trap for me! (*Runs back into bathroom.*)

SHE

(*Holding bottle up, puzzling over contents*)
Michael, wait a minute! (SHE *is interrupted by the sound
of his gargling*) I know! Well, this is the limit!

HE

(*Re-enters, wiping mouth with towel*)
What?

SHE

Do you remember, three years ago, that he had to take a
spoonful of cod liver oil every night and that he didn't want
to take it in my presence? Of course I measured the bottle
every morning, but he poured it into this!

HE

Agnes, do you mean to say that that stuff I swallowed is
three years old?

SHE

The little monkey! Oh, now I am going to wait till he
gets home!

HE

I think perhaps we'd better call the doctor. This stuff must be putrid by now.

SHE

You'll have to speak to him, Michael. This is one time that you'll have to speak to him. I . . .
(*Hears something*)
Michael, there he is!
(*Rises, goes to door.* HE *rushes to door, stops, returns to bench and picks up riding crop. Starts out.* SHE *stops him.*)
No, Michael, not that! Don't go that far!

HE

Three-year-old cod liver oil! (HE *whips the air with the riding crop. Exits.* SHE *listens for a moment, very worried. Then she runs into the bathroom and leaves the bottle there. Re-enters, to door, listens, goes down to bench at foot of bed and sits on end of it, all the while muttering to herself.* HE *appears in the doorway, dejectedly holding his riding crop in his hand.* HE *looks offstage, incredulously.* SHE *turns to him.*)

SHE

Well, what did you say?

HE

(*Closes door; distracted, turns to her*)
I beg your pardon?

SHE

What did you *say* to him?

HE

Oh—er—"Good morning."

SHE

Is that all?

HE

Yes.

SHE

Well, I must say! To go through all this rigmarole and then to end up with . . . I honestly think you could have said something more.

HE

(*Sits on sofa*)

I couldn't.

SHE

Why not?

HE

He was wearing a top hat.
(HE *makes a helpless gesture and rests his head in his hands.* SHE *laughs, crosses to him and puts her arms about him, then kisses him on the top of his head.*)

Curtain

ACT THREE

ACT THREE

SCENE I

1913. Late afternoon.

*The same bedroom. The bed canopy has been changed, as
have the drapes and articles of furniture. It is all in more con-
servative taste now.*

As the curtain rises, SHE *is seated at the dressing table,
holding a wedding bouquet that matches her gown and hat.
After a moment,* HE *is heard humming the Wedding March.*

HE
(From dressing room)

Agnes! (*Hums a bit more, then whistles for her.* HE *enters,
arranging his smoking jacket. Goes to foot of bed, humming
again. Sees her*) Oh, there you are. Your hat still on? Agnes!

SHE
(Starts)

Yes?

HE

Hey! Are you asleep?

SHE
(Sighs and smiles absently)

Yes . . .

HE

Come on, darling. The only thing to think is: little children grow up. Let's be glad she ended up so well.

SHE

Yes . . .

HE

Thank God, Robert is a boy. I couldn't stand to go through that a second time, to see my child abducted by such a . . . Oh, well, love is blind.

SHE
(*Putting down bouquet*)
Michael.

HE

Yes? (*Opens humidor and picks up pipe*) What is the matter with you? The whole day long you've been so . . . so strange.

SHE

How?

HE

You aren't ill, are you?

SHE

No.

HE

That's all right then. (*Starts filling his pipe*) What did you want to say?

SHE

Today is the first day of Lizzie's marriage.

HE

It is. And?

SHE

And the last day of ours.

HE

Beg pardon?

SHE

I waited to tell you, perhaps too long. I didn't want to spoil your fun.

HE

My *fun*?

SHE

Yes. I haven't seen you so cheerful for ages.

HE

Well . . . I'm . . . For your sake I have made a fool of myself. For your sake I have walked around all these days with the face of a professional comedian, with a flower in my buttonhole and death in my heart! Do you know what I would have liked to do? To hurl my glass in the pie face of that bore, take my child under my arm—and as for that couple of parents-in-law . . . (*Looks heavenward*) And now you start telling me you didn't want to spoil my fun! (*Searches pockets for match.*)

SHE

With the information that I am going away.

HE

You are what . . .

SHE

I'm going away.

HE

Huh?

SHE

Away.

HE

How do you mean?

SHE

Can't you help me just a little by understanding quickly what I mean?

HE

But, darling . . .

SHE

Michael, I'll say it to you plainly once, and please try to listen quietly. If you don't understand me after having heard it once, I'll . . . I'll have to write it to you.

HE

But, darling, we needn't make such a fuss about it. You want to have a holiday now the children have left the house.

What could be more sensible? No need to announce it to me like an undertaker.

SHE

Not for a holiday, Michael—forever.

HE

You want to move into another house?

SHE

I want to go away from *you*.

HE

From me?

SHE

Yes.

HE

You want to . . . visit friends, or something?

SHE

Please, darling, stop it. You knew ages ago what I meant; please don't try and play for time. It makes it all so . . . so difficult.

HE

I don't know a damn thing. What have I done?

SHE

Nothing, nothing. You are an angel. But I am . . . not.

HE

Agnes, what is the matter with you?

SHE

I would appreciate it if you would stop asking me what is the matter with me. There never has been anything the matter with me, and there couldn't be less the matter with me now. The only thing is, I can't . . .

HE

Can't what?

SHE

Die behind the stove, like a domestic animal.

HE

Good Heavens . . .

SHE

You wouldn't understand. You are a man. You'll be able to do what you like until you are seventy.

HE

But my dear good woman . . .

SHE

I won't! Today I stopped being a mother; in a few years' time, perhaps next year even, I'll stop being a woman.

HE

And that's what you don't want?

SHE

I can't help it. That happens to be the way a benevolent Providence arranged things.

HE

But, darling, then it's madness.

SHE

I want to be a woman just once, before . . . before I become a grandmother. Is that so unreasonable?

HE

But my angel . . .

SHE

For Heaven's sake, stop angeling me! You treat me as if I were sitting in a wheelchair already. I want to live, can't you understand that? My life long I have been a mother; my life long I've had to be at somebody's beck and call; I've never been able to be really myself, completely, wholeheartedly. No, never! From the very first day you have handcuffed me and gagged me and shut me in the dark. When I was still a child who didn't even know what it meant to be a woman, you turned me into a mother.

HE

But, darling, Robert is only . . .

SHE

No, not through Robert, not through Lizzie, through yourself, your selfishness, your . . . Oh, Michael. (*Puts her hand on his shoulder*) I didn't intend to say all this, honestly, I didn't. I only wanted to be honest and quiet and nice about it, but . . . but I can't help it. I can't! The mere way you look at me, now, this very moment! That amazement, that heartbreaking stupidity . . . Don't you feel yourself that there is nothing between us any more in the way of tenderness, of real feeling, of love; that we are dead, as dead as doornails,

that we move and think and talk like . . . like puppets?
Making the same gestures every day, the same words, the
same kisses . . . Today, in the carriage, it was sinister. The
same, the same, everything was the same; the coachman's
boots behind the little window, the sound of the hooves on
the pavement, the scent of flowers, the . . . I wanted to throw
open the door, jump out, fall, hurt myself, I don't know what
. . . only to feel that I was alive! I, I, not that innocent, gay
child in front, who was experiencing all this for the first
time, who played the part I had rehearsed for her . . . but I
couldn't. I said "yes" and "no" and "darling" and "Isn't it
cold," but I heard my own voice, and saw my own face mir-
rored in the little window, in the coachman's boots, like a
ghost, and as I put my hat straight, to prove to myself that
I wasn't a ghost, driving to my own burial, I remembered how,
twenty-three years ago, I had looked at myself in exactly the
same way, in the same window perhaps, to see if my bridal veil
. . . (HER *voice breaks;* SHE *covers her face with her hands;
goes up onto dais and falls onto bed, weeping.* HE *rises, puts
his pipe into his pocket, goes up onto dais and puts his hands
on her waist*) No! Don't touch me! (*Sits up, gets handkerchief from bedtable drawer and wipes her eyes*) I don't want
to, I don't want to blame you for anything. You've always
been an angel to me; you've always done whatever you could,
as much as you could . . . (HE *sits on bed*) although you
never opened a door for me, always got on the streetcar first,
never bought me anything nice . . . Oh, yes, I know, darling,
you have given me many beautiful presents. But something
real—if it had only been one book you didn't want to read
yourself; or one box of chocolates you didn't like yourself, but
nothing. Absolutely nothing. (*Shows him her hands*) Look, just
look! Only wrinkles and a wedding ring, and a new cash book
for the household every year. (*He takes her hand, raises it to his
lips, kisses the palm of her hand*) No, Michael. That's so easy,

so mean, really. You've always known how to make that one little gesture, say that one little word . . . but now it doesn't work any more. This is what I've been trying to tell you all along. It's the most difficult part of all, and I don't know if I . . . No, I can't.

HE

Say it.

SHE

I'm afraid—I think—I'm sure I don't love you any more. I don't say this to hurt you, darling, honestly I don't. I only want you to understand. Do you? Do you a little?

HE

Yes. I think so.

SHE

I even remember the moment I realized I didn't love you. One clear, terrible moment.

HE

When was that?

SHE

About a month ago, one Sunday morning, in the bathroom. I came in to bring you your coffee and you were rubbing your head with your scalp lotion. I said something about that boy's poems that you had given me to read; I don't remember what I said—and then you said, "I could tell him where to put them" . . . with both hands on your head. (*Puts*

hands on her head) And then . . . then it was suddenly as
if I were seeing you for the first time. It was horrible.

HE
(*After a silence*)
Where had you thought of going?

SHE
Oh, I don't know. I thought a room in a boarding house
somewhere.

HE
Not a trip, abroad for instance?

SHE
Good Heavens, no.

HE
Why not?

SHE
Because I don't feel like it . . . (*Turns to him*) You don't
think that I . . . that there is something the matter with me?

SHE
No.

SHE
Do you understand now why I *must* go away?

HE
Well, if I were to come into the bathroom with my head
full of love lyrics, like you, only to see you rubbing your face

with skin food or shaving your arm pits, I don't think I'd
have been overcome by any wave of tenderness for you . . .
but I wouldn't go and live in a boarding house.

SHE

That was not the point. The point was what you said.

HE

"I could tell him where to put them." H'm. You're sure
that was the point?

SHE

Why?

HE

Who wrote those poems you were talking about?

SHE

Well, that boy . . . that boy, who keeps asking you what
you think about his work.

HE

You liked what he wrote, didn't you?

SHE

Oh, yes. I thought it young, promising . . . honestly. It
had something so . . . so . . .

HE

So . . . well?

SHE

Well, what?

HE

I seem to remember this same description, twenty-three years ago.

SHE

You aren't trying to tell me that I'm . . . ? I won't say another word to you! The very idea that I, with a boy like that, such a . . . such . . . It's just that the boy has talent! At least as much as you had, when you were still rhyming about gazelles with golden horns.

HE

I was rhyming about you.

SHE

He must be rhyming about somebody as well, but . . .

HE

Of course he is. About you, too.

SHE

Me?

HE

What did he write on the title page? "Dedicated in reverent admiration to the woman who inspired my master." Well, I have been his master only insofar that I wrote him a letter: "Dear Sir, I have read your poems twice. I would advise you to do the same." Still, I don't know. Perhaps I'm growing old-fashioned. After all, he's new school and all that. I should like to read those poems again. Have you got them here?

SHE

Yes.

HE

Where are they?

SHE

(*Gets poems from lower drawer of bedside table; walks to foot
of bed and starts to hand him the poems, then stops*)
You aren't going to make fun of them, are you?

HE

(HE *takes out glasses, puts them on, takes poems from her*)
Fun? Why should I? I think this occasion is serious enough
for both of us to find out what exactly we're talking about.
Perhaps you're right. Perhaps I need this lesson. Well, let's
have it.
   (*Reads the title*)
"Flashing Foam—Jetsam on the Beach of Youth"
H'm. That seems to cover quite a lot.
First Sonnet: "Nocturnal Embrace."

SHE

Michael, if you're going to make a fool of this poor boy
who is just starting, only because you. . . .

HE

Who is doing the starting here? Me! After thirty years I'm
just starting to discover how difficult it is to write something
that is worth reading, and I *shall* write something worth reading one day unless . . . well, "Nocturnal Embrace."
   (*Reads*)
         "We are lying in the double bed,
            On the windows have thrown a net
               The dead leaves of an acorn tree."

Do you understand why it has to be an acorn tree? Why not an oak?

SHE

Because it's beautiful. Because it gives atmosphere.

HE

I see. I'm sorry.
　　(HE *reads*)
　　　　"From a church tower far unseen,
　　　　A solemn bell strikes twelve."
Well, now that rhyme could definitely be improved.
　　　　"From a church tower far unseen,
　　　　A solemn bell strikes just thirteen."
　　(SHE *doesn't answer.* HE *reads on*)
　　　　"Strikes twelve,
　　　　O'er the darkened fields,
　　　　The silent sea.
　　　　But then we start and clasp
　　　　A frightened, sickening gasp,
　　　　For a foot has stopped behind the door."
Now this I understand. No wonder they are startled. Suppose you're just busy clasping each other, and then a foot walks along the corridor and stops right outside your door . . .
　　(HE *shudders.*)

SHE

I'm not laughing, if that's what you're after.

HE

That's not what he was after in any case, but let's see how it ends.

(HE *reads*)
    "For a foot has stopped behind the door.
    Silence. Thumping. It's our hearts
    Waiting with our breath . . ."
Wondering where the other foot's got to, I suppose . . .

SHE

Michael, please stop it!

HE

Why? Am I his master or am I not? And has he had the
cheek to dedicate this bad pornography to my Agnes or has
he not?

SHE

He meant it for the best.

HE

Oh, now, did he really? Do you call that for the best, to
turn the head of a woman, the best wife any man could wish
himself, at the moment when she's standing empty-handed because she imagines her job is over? To catch her at a time
when she can't think of anything better to do than to become
young again and wants to start for a second time fashioning
the first damn fool at hand into a writer like me?

SHE

But you don't need me any more.

HE

Oh, no? Well, let me tell you something. People may buy
my books by the thousands, they may write me letters and
tell me how I broke their hearts and made them bawl their
damn heads off, but I know the truth all right. It's *you* who
make me sing . . . and if I sing like a frog in a pond, it's
not my fault.

(SHE *is so amused and relieved that she cries and laughs at the same time. The laughter gets the upper hand.*)

SHE

Oh, Michael!

HE

What are you laughing at?

SHE
(*Sitting on sofa beside him*)
Oh, Michael . . . I'm not laughing. . . . I'm not laughing.
(SHE *embraces him and sobs on his shoulder.*)

HE
(*Comforts her like a man who suddenly feels very tired*)
I'll be damned if I understand that.
(HE *rests his head on her shoulder.*)

Curtain

ACT THREE

Scene II

1925. Dawn.

Same bedroom, twelve years later. It is apparent that they are moving out—pictures have been taken off the walls, leaving discolored squares on the wallpaper; a step-ladder leans against the wall of archway; all drapes have been removed with the exception of the bed canopy and spread on the four-poster which is the only piece of furniture remaining in the room. Several large suitcases, packed and closed.

AT RISE, HE is heard messing about in the bathroom. Then HE comes out, humming and carrying toilet articles. HE goes to the suitcases, finds them shut, carries the stuff to the bed. HE goes again to the suitcases, opens one. It is full. HE slams the lid shut and fastens the locks, at the same time noticing that a small piece of clothing is left hanging out. HE disregards it and drags a second case on top of the first one, opens it, finds that it is fully packed as well. However, HE re-arranges the contents to make room for his toilet articles. As HE starts back to bed, he again notices the piece of clothing hanging out of the bottom case. HE looks toward door, then leans down and rips off the piece of material, puts it in his pocket and walks up onto dais. HE picks up his toilet articles from the bed, turns, then drops them on the floor. HE mutters, "Damn!" and gets down on his hands and knees to pick them up. At that moment, when HE is out of sight of the door, SHE comes in carrying the little "God Is Love" pillow. The moment SHE realizes he is there, SHE quickly hides the pillow behind her back.

105

SHE

What are you doing?

HE
(*Rises*)

Packing.

SHE
(*Picks up knitting bag from floor at foot of bed and puts it with the suitcases*)
Well, hurry up, darling. The car comes at eight and it's almost twenty of. What have you been doing all this time?

HE

Taking down the soap dish in the bathroom.

SHE

The soap dish? What on earth for?

HE

I thought it might come in useful.

SHE

But, darling, you mustn't. It's a fixture.

HE

Nonsense. Anything that is screwed on isn't a fixture. Only things that are nailed.

SHE

That's not true at all. The agent explained it most carefully. Anything that's been fixed for more than twenty-five years is a fixture.

HE
(Hands her the soap dish)
Then I'm a fixture, too.

SHE
Don't be witty, darling. There isn't time.

HE
(Seeing little pillow under her arm)
Hey! (SHE *stops*) We don't have to take that little horror
with us, do we?

SHE
No.
    (Exits into bathroom.)

HE
(Picks up part of his toilet things)
What about the bed?

SHE
(Offstage)
What?

HE
Are you going to unmake the bed or have we sold the
blankets and the sheets with it?
    (Starts packing toilet things.)

SHE
(Offstage)
What is it, dear?

HE
Have we only sold the horse or the saddle as well?

SHE

(*Re-enters, holding the little pillow*)
Horse, what horse?

HE

What's to become of those things? (SHE *still does not under-stand*) Have we sold the bed clothes or haven't we?

SHE

Oh, no, dear. Only the spread. I'll pack the rest.
(*Puts little pillow under arm and strips pillow cases.*)

HE

In what? These suitcases are landmines. Why are you nurs-ing that thing?
(SHE *mumbles something and tucks little pillow more firmly under her arm.* HE *goes up to her*)
Just what are you planning to do with it?

SHE

I thought I'd leave it as a surprise.

HE

A surprise?

SHE

Yes, for the new tenants. Such a nice young couple.
(*Places pillow at the head of the bed.*)

HE

Have you visualized that surprise, may I ask?

SHE

Why?

HE

Two young people entering the bedroom on their first night of their marriage, uncovering the bed and finding a pillow a foot across with "God Is Love" written on it.

SHE

(*Picks up rest of toilet articles and newspaper from bed. Puts them down on dais, the newspaper on top*)
You've got nothing to do with it.

HE

Oh, I haven't, have I? Well, I have. I've only met those people once, but I'm not going to make a fool of myself.

SHE

But, darling . . .

HE

There's going to be no arguing about it, and that's final.
(*Snatches pillow and throws it on trunk. Mutters*)
God Is Love!

SHE

(*Stripping blanket and sheets from bed*)
All right. Now, why don't you run downstairs and have a look at the cellar?

HE

Why?

SHE

(*Stuffs bed linen in pillow case*)
To see if there's anything left there.

HE

Suppose there is something left there, what do you suggest
we do with it? Take it with us? You don't seem to realize
that the apartment won't hold the stuff from one floor of this
house.

SHE

Please, darling, don't bicker. We agreed that it was silly to
stay on here with all these empty rooms.

HE

But where are we going to put all this stuff?

SHE

Now, I've arranged all that. Why don't you go down and
see if there's anything left in the wine cellar?

HE

Ah, now you're talking.

(HE *goes out.* SHE *twirls the pillow case tight and leaves
it by the suitcases. Picks up the "God Is Love" pillow,
returns to the bed, and places it on top of the regular
bed pillows, then stands back and admires it. With one
hand on bedpost,* SHE *glances over the entire bed and
smiles fondly. Then straightens the spread, moves
around to side, smoothes out the cover, goes to foot of
bed, stops, hears him coming; walks around again and
quickly covers the "God Is Love" pillow with spread.*)

HE

(*Entering with champagne bottle*)

Look what I've found!

SHE

(*Going to foot of bed and arranging the cover there*)

What?

HE

Champagne! (*Blows dust from bottle*) Must be one that was left over from Robert's wedding.

SHE

Oh.

HE

Have we got any glasses up here?

SHE

Only the tooth glasses.

HE

(*Sits on edge of bed*)
All right, get them.

SHE

You aren't going to drink it now?

HE

Of course. Now, don't tell me this is a fixture!
(*Tears off foil from bottle.*)

SHE

But, darling, we can't drink champagne at eight o'clock in the morning.

HE

Why not?

SHE

We'll be reeling about when we get there. That would be a nice first impression to make on the landlady!

HE

I'd be delighted. I'd go up to that female sergeant major and say, "Hiya! Hah! Hah!"

(*Blows his breath in her face as in the First Act. The memory strikes them both. They stay for a moment motionless.* SHE *pats his cheek.*)

SHE

I'll go get those glasses.

(SHE *exits into bathroom.*)

(HE *rises, throws the foil into the wastebasket at foot of bed, goes to suitcases and puts bottle on floor. Goes back to bed and looks for the rest of his toilet articles.* HE *pulls back the spread, picks up the "God Is Love" pillow, looks under it, tosses it back, looks under the other pillows, then suddenly realizes that the "God Is Love" pillow has been put back in the bed. Picks it up and calls:*)

HE

Agnes.

SHE
(*Offstage*)

What?

HE

Agnes.

SHE
(*Re-enters carrying towel and two glasses*)

What? Oh . . .

(SHE *is upset when she sees what it is, and very self-conscious.*)

HE

Agnes, did you put this back in the bed?

SHE

(*Standing at bathroom door*)
Yes.

HE

Why, for Heaven's sake?

SHE

I told you . . . I wanted to leave something . . . friendly for that young couple . . . a sort of message.

HE

What message?

SHE

I'd like to tell them how happy we'd been—and that it was a very good bed . . . I mean, it's had a very nice history, and that . . . marriage was a good thing.

HE

Well, believe me, that's not the message they'll read from this pillow. Agnes, we'll do anything you like, we'll write them a letter, or carve our initials in the bed, but I won't let you do this to that boy . . .

SHE

Why not? (SHE *puts glasses and towel on floor beside knitting bag, takes little pillow from him and goes up to bed*) When I found this very same little pillow in this very same bed on the first night of our marriage, I nearly burst into tears!

HE

Oh, you did, did you? Well, so did I! And it's time you heard about it! When, on that night, at that moment, I first saw that pillow, I suddenly felt as if I'd been caught in a world of women. Yes, women! I suddenly saw loom up behind you the biggest trade union in the world, and if I hadn't been a coward in long woolen underwear with my shoes off, I would have made a dive for freedom.

SHE

That's a fine thing to say! After all these years . . .

HE

Now, we'll have none of that. You can burst into tears, you can stand on your head, you can divorce me, but I'm not going to let you paralyze that boy at a crucial moment.

SHE

But it isn't a crucial moment!

HE

It is *the* crucial moment!

SHE

It is not! She would find it before, when she made the bed. That's why I put it there. It is meant for her, not for him, not for you, for her, from me!
(*Puts little pillow on bed as before.*)

HE

Whomever it's for, the answer is NO! (HE *takes the little pillow and puts it on the trunk again.* SHE *pulls the spread up over the bed pillows*) Whatever did I do with the rest of my toilet things?

(SHE *picks them up from floor by bed, goes to him, hands them to him, puts newspaper in wastebasket, sets basket down near arch.* HE *is very carefully packing his things. When he is finished, he closes the lid to the suitcase, tries to lock it, but doesn't succeed.*)

HE

You'll have to sit on this with me. I'll never get it shut alone. (SHE *sits down beside him*) Now, get hold of the lock and when I say "Yes," we'll both do—that. (HE *bounces on the suitcase*) Ready? Yes! (*They bounce.* HE *fastens his lock*) Is it shut?

SHE

(*Trying to fix catch*)

Not quite.

HE

What do you mean, not quite? Either it's shut or it isn't.

SHE

It isn't.

HE

All right. Here we go again. Ready? Yes! (*They bounce again*) All right?

SHE

Yes.

HE

(*Picks up champagne bottle*)

Now, do we drink this champagne or don't we?

SHE

(*Picks up glasses, towel, packs them in knitting bag*)
No.

HE

All right. I just thought it would be a nice idea. Sort of round
things off. (*Puts champagne bottle back on floor*) Well, what
do we do? Sit here on the suitcase till the car comes, or go
downstairs and wait in the hall?

SHE

I don't know.
        (HE *looks at her, then at the little pillow on trunk, then
        smiles at her anger.*)

HE

It's odd, you know, how after you have lived in a place for
so long, a room gets full of echoes. Almost everything we've
said this morning we have said before . . . It's the bed, really,
that I regret most. Pity it wouldn't fit. I wonder how the next
couple will get along. Do you know what he does?

SHE

He's a salesman.

HE

A salesman, eh? Well, why not? So was I. Only I realized
it too late. The nights that I lay awake in that bed thinking
how I'd beat Shakespeare at the game . . . .

SHE

Never mind, darling, you've given a lot of invalids a very
nice time.
        (*In his reaction, as* HE *turns to reply, the doorbell rings.*)

(HE *rises and looks out window. He goes to door, opens it.* SHE *rises and turns top suitcase up.* HE *puts bed linen under left arm, picks up top suitcase in left hand.* SHE *turns up the other suitcase and* HE *picks that one up in his right hand; turns to go.* SHE *quickly gets the knitting bag, stops him and tucks it under his right arm.* HE *exits.*

SHE *picks up purse, gloves, from off of trunk, then quickly takes the little pillow and goes to bed but stops suddenly, hearing him return, and hides the pillow under her coat.* HE *goes to trunk, leans over to grasp its handle, sees that the little pillow is not there, but proceeds to drag the trunk out. At the door, as* HE *swings trunk around,* HE *looks back at her.* SHE *is standing, leaning against the bedpost, pulling on her gloves. As soon as* HE *is out of sight,* SHE *hurriedly puts the pillow back into the bed and covers it.*

HE *re-enters, wearing his hat, picks up bottle of champagne, goes up to bed, drops hat on foot of bed, flings back the covers, picks up the little pillow and throws it to her side of the bed; then throws the bottle of champagne down on the pillow on his side and flips the spread back into place.* HE *picks up his hat and goes to her. They stand there for a moment, looking about the room.* HE *puts his hat on, smiles, leans down and hesitantly, but surely, picks her up.* SHE *cries, "Michael!"* HE *stands there for a moment, kisses her, then turns and carries her out of the room.*)

Curtain